A Dangerous Devotion

2004-2005 NMI
MISSION EDUCATION RESOURCES

✳ ✳ ✳

READING BOOKS

A DANGEROUS DEVOTION
Ordinary People in Extraordinary Adventures
by Carol Anne Eby

AFRICAN MOONS
by Juanita Moon

BEHIND THE VEIL
Taking Christ to Pakistanis
by Dallas Mucci

TAKIN' IT TO THE STREETS
by Joe Colaizzi

THE ROOKIE
Reflections of a New Missionary
by Tim Crutcher

WORDS OF LIFE AND LOVE
World Mission Literature Ministries
by Keith Schwanz

✳ ✳ ✳

ADULT MISSION EDUCATION RESOURCE BOOK

THE MISSION CALL
Edited by Wes Eby

A Dangerous Devotion

Ordinary People in Extraordinary Adventures

by

Carol Anne Eby

NPH

Nazarene Publishing House
Kansas City, Missouri

10   9   8   7   6   5   4   3   2   1

Dedication

To Tim and Melanie,
my missionary children,
whose lives and dedication to God
reflect *a dangerous devotion*
that truly sets them apart
as two very special instruments
in the hands of God.

Contents

Carol Anne Eby and her husband, Lee, were missionaries in Papua New Guinea for 20 years. After returning from the mission field, she was an English professor at Trevecca Nazarene University for 18 years, retiring in 2000. Lee retired last year from World Relief as the director responsible for refugee and new immigrant resettlement in Tennessee. The Ebys reside in Nashville.

Carol Anne and Lee have four children: Mark, who is on staff at the University of California, Los Angeles; Lee Ann, wife of Christian fiction writer, Ted Dekker; Timothy, a pilot, who with his wife, Michelle, are missionaries in East Africa; and Melanie with her husband, Larry Jones, serve in missions in northeastern Brazil.

As a freelance author, Carol Anne has written *To See, To Build, To Win: Volunteers for the Kingdom,* an NMI mission book for 2000-01 and *Wanda,* the story of missionary Wanda Knox, an NMI mission book 1991-92. She has also written for the *Adult Mission Education Leader's Guide* and *Come Ye Apart.*

Prologue

Missionaries are often looked upon as super saints. They would be the first to tell you that they are very human and feel and deal with the same emotions that all of us do—disappointment, discouragement, fear, loneliness, temptation, etc. Missionaries would claim to be ordinary people who have placed their God-given talents and lives into the hands of the Creator who with His divine touch has transformed the ordinary into extraordinary adventures of faith. The following stories reflect courage, patience, perseverance, compassion, faith, and love accompanied with *a dangerous devotion*, which perhaps is the quality that truly sets the missionary apart.

My childhood was deeply impacted by the stories told by missionaries who with God's divine call shaped my future. Today, I have my own stories, but I am also deeply indebted to my missionary colleagues, my friends, and my children who shared their own stories to bring this book into existence. Special thanks go to Melanie Jones, Carolyn Hannay, Peggy Perry, Tim Eby, Sharon Buess, Tom Riley, Ruth Kinnersley, and Geneva Silvernail for sharing their inspiring experiences that reflect *a dangerous devotion*, which can only come from God.

I also want to thank Wes Eby, my editor, for his encouragement and tireless effort in perfecting our writing.

God's Plans Are Best
Carol Anne Eby

My husband, Lee, closed the book he was reading with an enthusiastic, "My, that's interesting, but I sure wouldn't want to go there!" The book was *The Call of New Guinea*, Sidney Knox's narration of the opening of the work of the Church of the Nazarene in New Guinea. However, five years later in God's timing, a young man who had answered God's call at age 12 to "declare God's glory among the heathen" (Ps. 96:3*a*, KJV) saw that call become a reality as he, with our young family, settled into a new way of life among the Tongeii people.

Lee was born in Miami, Florida, and to a city boy used to skyscrapers, paved streets, and a beautiful beach bordering the Atlantic, Papua New Guinea was a sharp contrast of rugged mountains, isolated and primitive. Our people in the Western Highlands were unknown to the modern world until Australian gold prospectors discovered them in the 1930s. With our two babies only 20 months and 3 months old, we often wondered if we had made a grave error in judgment in accepting this missionary assignment. But we were assured again and again that this truly was God's plan for our lives.

A few months after arriving, Lee was riding in a jeep with the mission director along a winding, treacherous road. Another call came into reality with the question, "Lee, how would you feel about beginning a Bible school to train pastors?" With his heart in his mouth as the jeep slid around hairpin corners and teetered on the edge of steep precipices, he answered, "I'd love the opportunity." Then he silently added a prayer, "Lord, if You just let me live to do so!"

━ ・ ━ ・ ━ ・ ━ ・ ━

How desperately we needed reliable men. And God supplied them.

━ ・ ━ ・ ━ ・ ━ ・ ━

It was just as well then that Lee didn't know the total of available textbooks was the four Gospels in Melanesian Pidgin . . . or his future would be filled with hours of developing materials, mimeographing by the hour, and sorting and binding books . . . or of the sore throats and loss of voice that would often come because oral instruction was necessary, at first, for the nonliterate students.

Fresh from the study of theology and church history, Lee learned that those studies would have to wait while he led his "babes in Christ" from the fear of the spirit world to a living, dynamic faith in a God who could cast out all fear and give perfect love. The exhortation of Paul to Timothy has been the compass that has guided Melanesia Nazarene Bible College (MNBC), as it is now named, throughout the years: "And the things you have heard me say in the presence of many witnesses entrust to reliable men who will also be qualified to teach others" (2 Tim. 2:2). Reliable men. This was the cry of our hearts back in 1963, for there were no pastors, no Sunday School teachers, no national church. How desperately we needed *reliable* men. And God supplied them.

Lee Eby with Bible school students, 1964

Now 40 years later, would Lee say it was worth all the sweat, blood, and tears? Oh, yes. Today MNBC has two campuses with more than a hundred students and has trained hundreds of pastors. God's plan for a young missionary who was privileged to plant the seed has resulted in an abundant harvest. It is a living testimony to the promise given not only to Jeremiah but to those today who put their trust in a living God who says, "'For I know the plans I have for you,' declares the LORD, 'plans to prosper you and not to harm you, plans to give you hope and a future'" (Jer. 29:11).

Magic or Magical?
Carol Anne Eby

Our family clustered around a gaily-bedecked tree on Christmas morning 1964. Lee and I delighted in the ohs and ahs of the children opening their gifts. As lovely holiday music filled the room, our hearts overflowed with love and happiness in the joy of another yuletide morn. Watching this scene, I thought, *Christmas is really the same all over the world.*

I went to the front windows to open the drapes and let the sunlight in, which revealed rows and rows of dark faces pressed against the panes, marveling at the sights within. For these people there would be no exchange of gifts, no carols in their homes, no holiday dinners. Christmas was just another day to toil in the sweet potato gardens, to trudge the jungle trails, to go on with a rather meaningless existence, most of them not yet knowing that Christ had been born to be their Savior. I knew then that Christmas is not always the same. Only for those who know the Savior is Christmas the same, wherever they may be.

Lee Ann, the Eby's oldest daughter in 1964

Bringing Christmas for the first time to an isolated part of the world was a unique experience. As young, green missionaries, we didn't realize how strange our familiar customs were to our New Guinean people. We also didn't know that the great joy we hoped to convey had actually turned into fear.

The magical aura of our celebration disintegrating into black magic dismayed us.

16

Months later our houseboy told us how that first Christmas really established our reputation as powerful witch doctors or "poison men," as they are called in New Guinea. Our holiday celebration was the main topic of conversation around campfires for many evenings. All the people were convinced that the white man's magic had produced the lovely green tree grown overnight in our living room. In New Guinea all trees are personally owned, and if one is cut down, the owner notes it. The men searched the forest, but all trees were accounted for. They didn't realize ours was artificial and had come out of our 44-gallon packing drum. To people who were constantly amazed by the simplest conveniences of running water, electric lights, ice, and even matches, colored flashing lights, artificial snow, delicate ornaments on a magical tree was almost more than they could comprehend. The magical aura of our celebration disintegrating into black magic dismayed us and reminded us again of the great task that lay ahead.

After that first Christmas, we held open house each year and invited our station workers and Bible college students in for the evening. As they watched us assemble our tree, we explained our holiday customs and shared the Christmas story so old to us, so new to them.

Gradually as the Christ of Christmas became real in their hearts and lives, Christmastime took on new meaning. New Guinea Christians began to develop their own celebration experiences. Churches were blanketed with crimson poinsettias, which grew like trees along the jungle paths. The people built a manger like a birthing nest borrowed from their naming rituals for a newborn and placed it in the church to welcome Baby Jesus. They loved to dramatize the Christmas story, especially the part about going to Bethlehem to pay taxes. This is part of New Guinea culture, as people go to pay their taxes annually when the Australian patrol officer calls out the names of each family. Since they identified so well with this event, the roll caller was a coveted part for those reenacting the drama. Church services were followed by a Christmas feast and a time of celebration.

No experience has ever quite equaled that of sharing the Christmas story for the very first time to someone who has never heard. Telling the glad tidings is truly a magical feeling.

Down in the Dumps
Melanie Jones

OK! I will admit I've probably said it. On a very bad day when I can't see the wood grain on my desk because of the pile of paperwork, the phone's rung a hundred times, and 10 people stopped in for unexpected visits, I may have exclaimed, "This is the dumps today!" I may have that feeling when I'm frustrated after the puppy had dug up the flowers once again, and I've rushed my two-year-old to the hospital again for stitches after one of her more active moments. But, today, I really was in the dump and found the experience to be one of the most moving of my life.

My husband, Larry, and I are responsible for a team of 15 development workers, of which 10 are North Americans and 5, Brazilians. The most enjoyable part of the job for me is visiting each member of the team at their work site often up to four hours away from our home office in Recife in northeastern Brazil. Today I went to visit Delphine.

Getting off the bus, the first thing I noticed was the smell. Delphine works with the *catadores*—people who sort through incoming refuse for recyclable items, such as plastic, glass, paper, aluminum, etc.—

at the Olinda city dump. The smell of rotting garbage permeates the air 24 hours a day. I crossed the road and carefully picked my way up the mud trail to the Anglican mission where Delphine was conducting a class on making recycled paper with a group of young people, who were making cards and envelopes out of paper they had made the week before. The students were motivated and excited about the possibilities of selling these items in an upcoming exposition. Delphine has faced opposition from the local population in giving value to recyclable material. Those who live near the dump and confront the smell and sight of the garbage dump do not value the recycled material. I admired her determination to keep at the job.

▬ ▪ ▬ ▪ ▬ ▪ ▬ ▪ ▬

This dangerous work continues nonstop day and night.

▬ ▪ ▬ ▪ ▬ ▪ ▬ ▪ ▬

At the end of the class, Delphine and I walked to her home about 10 minutes away. We chose our steps carefully, avoiding the open stream of runoff drainage. I seriously asked Delphine if her vaccinations were current. After lunch of rice and beans at a small nearby restaurant, Delphine led me back to the dump to introduce me to some of the people she works with. We walked up a large dirt hill, which I later realized was one of four large covered areas of rubbish. From our vantage point on top, we saw the other three mountains of refuse in various stages of decomposition. One is being built little by little as the city garbage trucks enter and dispose their loads. In between the truck and the bulldozer that pushed the garbage up the hill are numerous *catadores*, trying to collect recyclables before being destroyed. This dangerous work continues nonstop day and night.

As we watched, a young woman, Luzia, came up to say "hi" to Delphine. We chatted a few moments, and then Luzia pointed out a pile of bags down the hill that she indicated were her collections. She was worried someone would steal them before she had a chance to sell them to a dealer. Delphine is working with an association of catadores to be able to skip this agent and as a group sell to

Delphine at the Olinda dump

those who buy recyclables. The dealers regularly cheat these destitute people by using dishonest weights and measurements. Luzia was eager to know how things were going with the association. After Delphine reminded her of some upcoming meetings, Luzia went back to work.

Delphine and I continued on farther into the dump, coming upon a small lake of putrid water with many bags of rubbish in and around it. There were clear signs of hospital waste that should have been buried but had just been discarded in a pile. Making our way around the lake we saw two pigs wallowing in the mud. We entered a tree-shaded area, the "home" for most of the catadores who live with their chickens, dogs, cats, and other animals. Shacks made from used wood, tin, and cardboard covered the area.

We stopped by one shack about the size of my living room that shelters a dozen people. I assumed that not all 12 are in this small space at the same time.

Moving on to another shack, we observed an eight-year-old boy taking care of his little brother. The father was working in the dump, and the mother was at the hospital with their baby sick with pneumonia. Delphine had taken them to the hospital, so she wanted to check on the infant's progress.

We made our way on through the settlement and then back to the entrance. Delphine was greeted all along the way by people she knows. She knows them, but officially they don't exist, as most recyclers have no legal documents, such as identity cards or birth certificates. Delphine has done much to accompany the recyclers on their path toward legalization and toward becoming citizens, being able to travel freely, vote, work, and become real citizens who can exercise their rights. Delphine and her family are ministering to the poorest of the poor at the Olinda dump. These children of God need our prayers.

I returned to my comfortable office overwhelmed by what I had seen. The needs are immense, but we keep at the work one day at a time. Yes, I'm sure I'll have more down-in-the-dumps days. But now it seems more like a holy place, as people like Delphine minister in the name of Christ so that people's broken lives will not just be recycled—but transformed!

Collision

Carolyn Hannay

Every schoolchild likes recess time. In fact, some call it their favorite "subject." Recess is especially fun for the children in Papua New Guinea with its perpetual springtime. The warm, sunny days beckon boys and girls to come outside and play.

On one of those glorious days, the children playing at the Banz Catholic school were delightfully happy. Salome, a petite 12-year-old, and her friends were enjoying a game of tag. The school yard echoed

Children playing at recess

with the girl's voices, laughing and yelling at each other as they darted back and forth across the playground.

Suddenly one of the girls bumped Salome, and they fell to the ground, giggling and unhurt—or so it seemed. Salome's friend quickly jumped up and ran off again but then turned in concern. Salome did not get up. The girls ran for the teacher who came and checked Salome for injuries, and although she found none thought it wise to take the girl to the Nazarene hospital about five miles distant. On the way Salome near tears took comfort in her teacher's concern. Though nothing seemed to be broken, the weakness in her legs did not allow her to walk.

Salome was seen in the emergency room by Dr. Jack Patton, who admitted her for observation. Salome with a big smile, bubbly personality, and patient demeanor quickly won the hearts of all the hospital staff.

Her legs' weakness slowly progressed up her body until she could not move her legs or arms. After several months of this paralysis, stealing away her energy and vitality, her young life seemed to be in jeopardy. Dr. Patton told the staff that if this paralysis reached her heart and lungs she would die.

We had lifted Salome to God in prayer, but now we realized that unless a miracle took place, this precious little girl would be destroyed by her strange malady. Missionary Ruth Blowers became Salome's special friend. Ruth often brought cookies and lemonade and fed the girl while sharing the gospel and encouraging her.

One Saturday night Ruth asked some nurses to join her in prayer for Salome's healing. We met, prayed, and read Scripture. Then going to Salome's bedside, we asked permission to pray for her.

"Oh, yes," she said with her ear-to-ear smile.

We quoted God's promises, read the Bible, and prayed. Returning to our homes with peace, we believed His Word and promises were for Salome.

— · — · — · — · —

We rejoiced, crying and laughing at the same time, as we knew God was doing something astounding in her life.

— · — · — · — · —

Sunday morning came early as I made my way to the hospital for duty. It was one of those hectic days. The hospital wards were busy, as many new patients were admitted. At noon, I rushed home for a quick lunch. When I bowed my head to say grace, God spoke to my heart: "Last night you asked Me to heal Salome, and you haven't been to see what I've done." I felt ashamed but reminded the Lord of how busy the hospital had been.

Gobbling down my food, I dashed back to the hospital and went straight to Salome's room.

Before she could say a word, I asked, "Salome, what did Jesus do for you last night?"

"Look," she said with a bright countenance. For the first time she moved the fingers on her right hand. We rejoiced, crying and laughing at the same time, as we knew God was doing something astounding in her life. Each day we watched with anticipation at her progress. Slowly but surely God completely restored her health.

Then came the day she was dismissed to go home, but not without a good-bye party from all the hospital staff and, of course, Aunt Ruth Blowers. God was faithful and another miracle was recorded.

Twenty years later after a long absence, I was privileged to return to Papua New Guinea on a Work

Salome as an adult

and Witness trip. I made a list of the people I really wanted to see again, and Salome was on that list. I inquired of her whereabouts from all the hospital staff who possibly remembered her. They told me she was married and lived on the other side of the big mountain. I felt sad knowing I could not find her.

On Saturday morning I wanted to experience the open-air market across the road from where we were staying and asked one of the other ladies on the team to accompany me. We made our purchase of fresh pineapples and started for home. Suddenly I heard a voice crying, "Miss Carolyn, Miss Carolyn!"

Turning to see who was calling, I looked into the smiling face of Salome. We laughed, hugged, and cried for joy. "Just last night," she said, "I was telling my husband about you. What a surprise!"

Salome had come to bring her child to the doctor and had stopped just briefly at the market. God in His goodness had healed her body many years ago, and now He orchestrated every detail for our reunion. I was able to witness again to her and pray for her family's salvation. What a caring and loving God we have. The day of miracles is not over.

Thanks, Lord, for the Celery

Carol Anne Eby

Glumly I stared out the window. Trees clustered
with golden bananas, bushes thick with flaming
poinsettias and hibiscus, and rows of sweet, juicy
pineapples stretched before me in a tropical par-
adise. But it was November, and I longed for crisp,
not balmy, breezes. I wanted to smell, not the sea,
but wood smoke wafting across the hills. And I
wanted to celebrate Thanksgiving with all the ceremony to which my family had been accustomed.

We were celebrating our first Thanksgiving
abroad as missionaries. This South Pacific nation
knew little or nothing about Pilgrims, Indians, and
harvest celebrations. Yet wanting to preserve cultural
traditions for our children, I decided to plan a traditional Thanksgiving dinner for our entire staff and
their families.

Enthusiastically I made lists, issued invitations,
planned the menu, and gathered supplies. The children enjoyed the excitement as we hung turkey
posters, made Pilgrim cutouts, and stuffed the cornu-
copia with sweet potatoes, corn, pineapples, bananas,

oranges, and guavas. Though not exactly traditional, it was colorful.

As I worked on the menu one day, I stood dejectedly by the window, for I realized the meal couldn't be just like one back home. I had bought some fat hens to take the place of the nonexistent turkeys. Pumpkin was a common vegetable, although the thought of putting pumpkin in a pie made our Australian friends nauseous. A box of medical supplies had arrived from the States, and tucked among the bandages—surely by some divinely inspired missionary president—were several cans of cranberry sauce. The meal was coming together. But one ingredient was missing that I felt was absolutely necessary. How could I make stuffing with no celery? Where could I find celery on a South Pacific island? My husband, Lee, laughed, thinking celery salt and sage would make anything turn out right.

———·———·———·———·———

I shrieked, joyfully enveloping her and the celery in a giant bear hug.

———·———·———·———·———

My desire for celery almost became an obsession. I yearned for it, dreamed about it, and even rather apologetically prayed about it. "Lord, I know we're not hungry. We're blessed with plenty of food. We have so much to be thankful for. But that special touch would make things perfect. I know it would be a miracle, but, Lord, You can do anything."

Thanksgiving Day dawned, and I was busy in the kitchen. Someone knocked on the door, and Lee answered it. Then with a huge grin, he said, "Honey, you're never going to believe this."

On our veranda stood a New Guinean woman with a string bag slung over her head. The bag contained the biggest, most beautiful celery stalks I'd ever seen.

"Missus, can you use this, or is it weeds?"

I shrieked, joyfully enveloping her and the celery in a giant bear hug. "Where, oh, where did you get it?"

Women carrying garden produce in string bags

Months earlier at a local trade store, she had picked up a packet of seeds placed there by an Australian patrol officer who hoped someone would experiment with a new food. She had planted the seeds in her garden, but the resulting plant was so different from anything she had produced before that she doubted its culinary value.

I hugged her, overpaid her, and sent her trotting off for more. I made the stuffing, added celery to Jell-O, stuffed celery sticks, and delivered extra bundles to our missionary and government friends throughout the valley. I also remembered again and again to say, "Thanks, Lord. Thanks for the celery and a Thanksgiving I will never forget!"

Angels in the Night

Peggy Perry

The African sun hovered at the top of the mountain as if reluctant to relinquish its scorching grip on the day. I said a silent prayer for God to let it hover just a little longer. We needed all the daylight possible for the journey. Twilight lasts only briefly in Africa, and I knew we would be plunged into darkness very soon. The reddish yellow ball touched the horizon and began to sink behind the mountain too quickly. Suddenly, orange, scarlet, and ocher flares streaked across the early evening sky like a silent fireworks display, as if God was announcing again, "I am alive forevermore." Wow! What a fantastic way to end this Easter day.

This glorious day had been filled with activities celebrating the gift of God to His children—victory over sin and death through Jesus Christ. It had begun with singers under our bedroom window at 4:00 A.M. singing the good news, "He is Risen." Later, people streamed into the mission from all directions, singing "He Arose" with a sound of triumph. Sunday worship is always long in Africa, and this day was no exception. We raced from one event to another with little time to pause for breath.

Given the long weekend, Good Friday through Easter, we had made plans for the teens on the mission to come home from boarding school. Nancy's parents had picked them up on Thursday afternoon after school; now it was my turn to take them back. If we were fortunate, we would arrive before midnight.

Dashing from the dinner table, my daughter Angela and I said quick good-byes and were on our way down the rough mountain road to Manzini. We were now racing against the clock, for we had to be at the border before it closed at 6:00 P.M. Benny and Aries were ready and with short farewells to their mother, Dr. Bajoyo, we raced to Nancy's house. We quickly placed everything and everyone tightly into the Volkswagen Golf and headed out with 400 miles to go.

Swaziland countryside

As we bumped down the narrow, rutted dirt road, clouds of red dust rose and pushed its way into the open windows. I had to watch carefully for the cattle and goats that loved to congregate on the open road. We arrived at the border just in time to meet the deadline. Passports and visas were in order. After the officers searched our car, we headed out again.

The roads were paved as we entered South Africa from Swaziland, so traveling was much easier. But with hours to go, I pushed the little car as hard as I dared. While driving conditions had greatly improved, I was most anxious about this particular stretch of our journey. Thugs and gangs in the area had recently robbed and killed a number of people, burning their bodies in their vehicles.

My responsibility was great: I had precious cargo to deliver safely to boarding school. I kept my eyes open wide, searching for any danger lurking in the darkness. Even though I noticed the red light on the dashboard blink at me from time to time, I was unaware of the danger. But when the headlights began to dim, I realized something dreadful must be wrong. The battery obviously was running down, so the alternator must not be functioning. *We are in real trouble*, I thought. *Soon we'll be out of power and come to a grinding halt.* I prayed desperately. Eventually the engine chugged its last, and we coasted to the side of the road.

I surveyed the area. No lights anywhere, no filling stations, no garages, or anything for miles. The tall cane fields along the road rose like giant walls in the dark night. The border was closed, and any people in their right minds would be tightly tucked into their homes by now.

If the kids were worried, they didn't show it. We decided a picnic seemed appropriate, so we found our flashlights, opened up the goodies we had brought for the journey, and enjoyed a feast on the hood of the car. While I joined in the fun, my eyes kept vigilant for any danger or help that might be forthcoming. I saw a dim light in the distance, a hint of reflection at first. Little by little it developed into a bright spot through the river of night. "Please, God, send an angel and not a thug!"

When the car pulled alongside us, I shared our situation with the lone driver who seemed friendly and who happened to have an extra battery in his boot (trunk). With the boys helping, he removed our dead battery and placed his extra one in our VW. It fit! We joined hands and prayed that God would make it work, and as I turned the starter, the car jumped to life. I agreed to stop by the workplace of our angel in the night and return the battery on my way home.

The kids resumed their singing and laughter while I resumed my concern. The battery was not new, and I wasn't sure how much power it had. Since the alternator was still not charging, we had to conserve power. With the boys hanging from the windows, they used two flashlights to show us the way. No cars came, so all we had to worry about was staying on the road. If we could make it to the next village, we could find help. We soon drained the battery on loan, and the VW stopped dead—again.

I wasn't sure about the "angel stuff," as he had a Colt 44 strapped to his hip.

With my head resting on the steering wheel, I reminded God of where we were—just in case He had forgotten. I thanked Him for the loaned battery that had gotten us this far but questioned why He had not let it last just nine more miles. As I prayed shouts rang out, "Aunty, Aunty, a car's coming!"

Down the black ribbon of road, lights raced toward us. The silver van flew by and raced on in spite of four flashlights frantically flashing on and off to signal our distress. Suddenly the vehicle braked, backed up, and my second angel in the night, an Afrikaans farmer, stepped out of the van. Yes, there was a garage in the town, he indicated, but nothing would be open at night.

My angel pulled behind our VW and pushed us right into the town and to the station. No one was stirring, but the Afrikaner found the night guard and explained our distress. A quick phone call but a long wait followed.

Then the third angel of the night in the form of an East Indian garage owner appeared. At first I wasn't sure about the "angel stuff," as he had a Colt 44 strapped to his hip. His plan? Go home with him to stay the rest of the night. I admit, the invitation was tempting. But looking at the gun and thinking about all the people who would be anxious if we did not arrive, I begged for his help. *Now!* He found the largest truck battery that would fit into my car. I paid a hefty price, he wished us luck, and we were rolling again.

With the new surge of power, we made good time to Durban and started the climb up the mountain on the final leg of the journey. The pull on the battery, however, became more evident as we clicked off the miles. By the time we reached Pietermaritzburg, we could hardly see. We chugged into the city and turned on the road to One Way Home for missionary kids. At the entrance the struggling VW puffed its last breath. The kids jumped out and pushed the VW in the gate and on to the drive. I gave the orders to unload, but the kids insisted on moving the car to protect it from thieves. At this point, I was so weary that I was tempted to leave the

Some of the school children in uniform
at One Way Home

keys in the ignition just to see if someone really would take it off my hands!

The next morning I awoke after everyone had already gone to school. Looking out the window, I discovered the Golf was still there covered with Swaziland red dust but otherwise looking healthy. Before long the vehicle was at a repair garage, and I had the treat of shopping for supplies to take back to Swaziland, as I didn't get to the big city very often.

At dinner that evening all 20 missionary kids heard the details of our exciting trip. To my surprise I was considered to be somewhat of an adventurous and heroic aunty, and all the other MKs decided to travel with me on the next trip to boarding school. "No more boring trips for us," they declared.

As we reviewed the journey, we were amazed to see how God worked in every situation. We prayed for our "angels in the night" and asked God to use our testimonies to witness to their hearts.

The next day I started out for Swaziland alone and wondered what surprises lay ahead of me. You see, I have always believed that walking with God is an adventure, and I look forward to what He has to teach me through life's experiences. I have learned that whether you walk, drive, fly, or float, you can trust Him for the journey. And when needed, He will send "angels in the night."

The Mud Holes of Mission Work

Tim Eby

I stared into the bright headlights of the Land Cruiser with disgust. Drenched to the skin with my pants stiff with mud and small rock and dirt clods in my boots securely submerged in the six inches of mud I was standing in, I looked up into the dark African sky and began to wonder why God had abandoned me. The drone of the men's voices surrounding the vehicle, suggesting one remedy after another in a language I couldn't understand, slipped into the night. I caught a glimpse of the missionary who had accompanied me as she slipped on the muddy roadside and grabbed the vehicle for support but still smiling bravely and clinging to a hope that somehow we were going to get out of this mess. The pastor of the local church sat on the edge of the road between the cornstalks, with head bowed and hands clutched together, praying for a solution. It became overwhelmingly apparent that all of us were in deep trouble.

What had begun as a great day was now ending in a frustrating and hopeless situation. The rain had begun about 30 minutes into the showing of the JESUS film in the remote village of Ihombe, dropping almost an inch of rain in less than two hours on the trail that wound down the mountain ridge back to Mbeya. The Land Cruiser had entered a short stretch of road with deep soft ruts where the tires tracked and huge stones in the center where the vehicle now rested securely on its frame. The tires had spun and spun, the vehicle going nowhere. The men pushed and shoved with all their effort, but no progress was made. For the past three hours, I had lain on my stomach in the mud and dug with my bare hands trying to remove the rocks from the car's frame.

As a missionary pilot for the Church of the Nazarene, it was ironic that I had traveled almost 600 miles to reach this area with the Good News using the JESUS film, and yet I was helpless to move beyond a 100-foot stretch of muddy road that now gripped the four-wheel drive vehicle tightly in its clutches.

It was Saturday night and almost the end of the crusade to Mbeya, Tanzania. God had blessed the showing of the film in Mbeya as 1,000 people crammed body to body, in standing-room-only style, to watch the life of Christ on film, and many gave their hearts to the Lord.

━ ∙ ━ ∙ ━ ∙ ━ ∙ ━

The Land Cruiser was stuck
in the mud before it had moved
100 feet from the church.

━ ∙ ━ ∙ ━ ∙ ━ ∙ ━

During the day pastors attended seminars to learn about the basic functions of the church. Most had no formal education and had not taken biblical studies, and yet they had been given the responsibility to carve out the Church of the Nazarene in the communities where they lived. Seven of the 17 pastors had come forward at the end of the week and been filled with the Holy Spirit and testified to the experience of entire sanctification. The week had been great, and this was the last assignment to show the *JESUS* film in Ihombe.

Getting ready to show the *JESUS* film

The team arrived safely, and 300 people packed the little church. Shortly after the film started, the rain began. By the end of the film it was past 8:00 P.M., and conditions outside were dark and wet. At the invitation to make a decision for Christ, eight people came forward under the light of the flickering kerosene lantern and dedicated their lives to the Lord.

The team praised the Lord for His goodness, broke down the equipment in the dark, and headed for the vehicle with haste. The Land Cruiser was stuck in the mud before it had moved 100 feet from the church. After almost an hour of digging, pushing, and finally physically raising the vehicle out of the ruts with long poles, the team was back on the main road and heading down the mountain.

Now, at 1:00 A.M. the vehicle was sunk again in the muddy ruts. After three hours in the rain and mud, everyone was discouraged. All efforts to remove the vehicle had been exhausted. "Kwisha!" I exclaimed, which means "it is finished." The eight members of the team and myself locked ourselves in the vehicle, prayed we would not be ambushed in the night, and drifted off to sleep in our wet clothes.

As dawn broke, I shook two of the pastors awake. Soon we started up the winding mountain path to a coffee plantation to get help. After nearly an hour of climbing and another half hour through rows of coffee trees, we stood on the doorstep of a German's home. Over a much-needed cup of coffee, we explained our predicament and asked for his help. Within an hour we had collected wood, ropes, jacks, shovels, a new battery, and a tractor to help pull out the Land Cruiser, and we all were headed back down the mountain. With the proper tools, we soon raised the vehicle out of the mud and set to cross the 100-foot stretch that seemed impossible to cross just hours before. Thanking the plantation owner again and again, our dirty but jubilant team burst into joyful song as we slid and bumped down the final stretch of road back into Mbeya.

In the months that followed, I was encouraged again and again as I thought of that experience. It is the mud holes of mission work that sometimes get us down. The devil would like nothing more than for us to give up and go home. He puts us in the mud holes of life, places the barriers to our progress, and watches us spin our wheels, going nowhere. The red tape of government bureaucracy, the cunning schemes of deceitful people, the lack of basic life supports (phones, water, and electricity) are all the work of the devil to stop God's kingdom from being built. But it is the power of the Holy Spirit that gives strength to carry on with a joyful spirit to over-come—even in the mud holes of life.

Tim Eby under his vehicle repairing a broken part

The Outlaws

Carol Anne Eby

Aching, tired muscles called me to rest. Though near midnight, a few small chores still needed to be finished.

The last few days had been a hectic routine of cooking, entertaining, talking, and playing as we celebrated our oldest son's last weekend home before returning to school. Because 13-year-old Mark attended a boarding high school 150 miles away over treacherous mountainous terrain and school holidays came only three times a year, the time at home was especially enjoyable.

I felt I had barely dozed when the air was rent with fierce barking from our dog. Though a lovable playmate to the children, Kim was a formidable watchdog who patrolled his turf with great possessiveness. No one stepped foot onto the property without caution. Drunks wandering past our mission compound, as well as prospective chicken thieves, had become cautious quickly.

As a frantic bark dissolved into a howl of pain, my husband jumped to his feet, grabbed the flashlight, and ran from the room. Anxiously I looked out the window. Our recently purchased bus, parked in the drive near the house to assure its safekeeping, now provided cover for the intruders. Fear gripped me as I saw a man crawl around the bus and then four accomplices joined him.

— · — · — · — · —

"Do you want to die?" the leader replied in menacing tones.

— · — · — · — · —

I hurried to warn Lee, but by this time he was already in the yard. Hearing him yell and a loud thump reverberate through the night, I dashed to the living room. Lee, having met a barrage of stones as he went out the front door, retreated swiftly, jumping back just as a stone slammed through the plywood wall with such force that it lodged there. Shaken, we looked at one another. Peering fearfully through the drapes, we could see the men, dressed in Levi's and motorcycle jackets, quite clearly in the moonlight. Quizzically, Lee and I looked at each other. *Were these university students from the coast on spring break*, we wondered, *who are bored and restless, wanting to get their excitement by terrorizing the countryside?*

Lee shouted out the door in the local language: "Who are you? What do you want?"

To our surprise the answer came in articulate English: "We are the outlaws, and we want your bus. Give us the key!"

Lee relaxed a bit. He was used to dealing with

college students. "I'm sorry, but I can't do that." His voice took on a bit more authority.

"Do you want to die?" the leader replied in menacing tones. "Give us the key, or we'll break into your house and kill your family!"

This was no schoolboy prank. We were dealing with desperate men bent on destruction. And we had no weapons in the house except a tire iron propped up in the corner left there after the afternoon's tire-changing chore. Lee grabbed it, but we both knew if those strong young thugs rushed the door, our weapon would be of little use.

We stood in the darkness feeling so helpless and alone. Then through the waves of fear that washed over me, I suddenly remembered. Never completely alone. God had promised to fight our battles, and He was there. My lips moved in silent prayer—for my four children who somehow were still miraculously asleep, for the Bible college students in their dorms a short distance away, for Lee and me, even for poor Kim who may have already had his throat cut. "O God, we need your help!"

Anxious moments passed as the men huddled over the bus engine frantically trying to cross the wires to start the ignition. Finally, in frustration, cursing and groaning with great exertion, they began pushing the bus down the drive. Lee grabbed the tire iron and slipped out the back door to awaken students to aid him in reclaiming the bus. Shortly, I heard a loud crash as the thieves finally gave up and shoved the bus over an embankment, fleeing on foot while hotly pursued by enraged stick-brandishing students.

Bible school bus, the object of the would-be thieves

The outlaws had too far a head start on the students. In the excitement of the chase and confusion in the darkness, the students lacked direction and lost the bandits in the night. Perhaps it was fortunate they had escaped, for the next day's report from a neighboring settlement revealed the grim statistics of the outlaws' night. They eventually stole a car, broke into a large trade store after stoning the owner's wife in his absence, and axed a priest, seriously wounding him after his efforts to stop their breaking and entering.

Why did the outlaws turn away from our door when they met no resistance? Or was there resistance? Long ago an Old Testament prophet reassured his panic-stricken servant when surrounded by invaders with these words: "Those who are with us are more than those who are with them. . . . O

LORD, open his eyes so he may see. . . . and he looked and saw the hills full of horses and chariots of fire all around . . ." (2 Kings 6:16b-17).

Could it be? Why not?

Blinded

Sharon Buess

It was an ordinary day . . . well, *ordinary* for the time and place, that is.

Our family was living in an apartment on the top floor of our seven-story mission building in Beirut, Lebanon. The structure housed not only our living quarters but an elementary and middle school, district offices, and a sanctuary used by two church congregations. Our building on a high hill over-looked a valley with the Mediterranean Sea in the background. The top floor provided the most exten-sive view of the valley.

But that unforgettable scene had become a war zone as incoming fire was being launched at our lo-cation. The country was engaged in civil war. One of the fighting groups had taken up a firing position in the building under construction next door to us. We were becoming accustomed to the sound of ma-chine-gun fire and rocket-propelled grenades being directed to the valley. Our building had become a sanctuary as we tried to ignore all that was happen-ing outside our gates.

That *ordinary* day occurred in February of 1978. As I was working in the kitchen, I looked down onto the school playground several stories below and noticed armed men in uniform. I phoned my husband, Larry, who was working in his office downstairs to let him know about the situation. A few minutes later, Larry hurried into the apartment and said intensely but calmly, "Get the children, and all of you go into our bedroom." When we had gathered, he told us that the men had asked to enter our building and go to the flat roof to shoot at something they could not see adequately from next door. As our building was the highest in the area, they could get the best position for firing at their target.

Falling on our knees, we asked the Lord for protection and to blind the men's eyes.

Larry had protested, of course. He told the intruders they would make our building a specific target for incoming fire. Fortunately, school was not in session at the time due to unsafe conditions. He explained to the men that this building was a home, school, and church. But ignoring his protests, the armed men demanded a key. They had guns; he didn't! He threw the key to them, and they started for the roof, warning Larry to stay away from the doors and windows because he would be in great danger.

Larry and I, along with our three children— Kent, 13; Michelle, 11; and Brent, 5—huddled in our bedroom. Falling on our knees, we asked the Lord

The Church of the Nazarene building in Beirut
(center with the cross)

for protection and to blind the men's eyes to whatever they were looking for. As waves of fear and anxiety washed over us, we believed in the power of a God who had blinded enemies in times past and who could still do it in today's battles. We arose from our knees reassured that God was in control.

Larry went to investigate and discovered the men coming down, shaking their heads, bewildered. They had been unable to see to launch their fire. Returning the key to Larry, they left our building.

We lived there approximately four more months before the danger became so great the church felt we must leave. Those men never returned, even when the fighting was most intense. We believe God honored our prayer and temporarily blinded the armed intruders. How thankful we were—and still are!

Death in the Hills
Tim Eby

I stared at the computer screen trying to bring
my mind to the task of writing a newsletter to update
family and friends about our ministry in East Africa.
As I reflected on my flying the last month over the
striking terrain of East Africa, I wanted to describe the
beauties of God's creation in this special place. I de-
sired to tell of picturesque Lake Victoria and the end-
less hills of Rwanda covered in deep jungle and banana
trees. I would love to describe the richly sculpted inlets
of Lake Kivu with its deep blue waters and rugged
shorelines that quickly fade into steeply rising volcanic
mountains along its shores. I wanted to express my excitement of flying to the remote strip at Cyangugu
near the border of the Republic of the Congo and re-
count the hair-raising adventure of crossing the border
into Zaire (now Democratic Republic of the Congo),
where traveling by road is still not safe due to the
rebels in the hillsides.

I could write about the bright faces of the young
people who sang with enthusiasm at the Church of
the Nazarene in Kigali, Rwanda. Because of former
President Clinton's arrival at the same airport at
which I landed, I could share the excitement of being

on the same tarmac with Air Force One. Yes, I could report the struggles of two young missionary families trying to make a difference in a country still reeling in the wake of civil war.

I could do all of these things and my reading audience would enjoy, be inspired, and motivated to support the work. But my mind and heart cannot erase the images I saw in the remote Catholic Church Memorial deep in the hills of Rwanda. I will never be able to remove that sight from my memory. The utter loss of human life haunts my mind. And so I begin to write.

— · — · — · — · —

The sense of evil lay heavy within the broken walls of the church.

— · — · — · — · —

We left the rejoicing atmosphere in the church of Kigali. Taking a Land Cruiser, we drove about an hour south of the city to a church that has been left as a memorial to the genocide of 1994—a time when neighbor killed neighbor for no other reason than a difference in tribal background and a perceived inequity of life status. The government estimates that during the 90-day period of this horrible event as many as 800,000 people were killed in this small country over ethnic differences.

Our destination was a church compound where many of the hunted tribe had come for refuge. Some 5,000 people were then surrounded and slaughtered like animals with the blunt force from machetes and simple farm tools. As we approached the site, we looked in horror at the dismembered bodies strewn across the compound and piled in heaps in the church. Everything has been left exactly as found when soldiers arrived to retaliate against these injustices. Women, children, and men met with the same ruthless violence. The crushed skulls and random limbs told the story of the terror that was dealt out the night of the killings. Deep gouges in the bark of the trees gave evidence to the victims that were made to stand against them before being decapitated or dismembered. In one area the skulls were stacked on tables by the hundreds. The pulpit had an open Bible with the skull of the priest still lying on it. The stench of death was everywhere; the sense of evil lay heavy within the broken walls of the church.

Somberly, we made our way to another area that was a mass grave now marked with rows of crosses. The burial ground is said to have at least 40,000 bodies, mostly unidentified. We crossed the river where thousands of bodies were dumped and left floating in the basin of Lake Victoria. The swamp around this area was the refuge for many who stayed submerged throughout the entire day and then scrounged along the banks at night to find food for survival.

As we made our way back to our vehicle, we were not sure what to say or think. Our silence in the vehicle as we returned to Kigali represented the quiet sadness each of us felt.

When I think of the scene of this crime, I can

only pray that somehow the evidence of such evil will help us in the future to never repeat such a senseless slaughter. I pray that our church takes the necessary steps to enter these people's lives and deliver them from sin's bondage.

I desire to be a part of any ministry that helps meet the needs of the thousands of widows and children that are the survivors. I hope we as a church can make a difference in Rwanda. I hope that my description doesn't offend you, and yet I hope it helps you realize that our battle isn't against flesh and blood but against the principalities and powers of evil.

Pray for the missionaries in Rwanda. When I fly there, I take them supplies like peanut butter, brown sugar, jelly, and good coffee. These ordinary items that people in the West take for granted help the missionaries' morale and give their kids something to look forward to. But they need your prayers more than anything and your encouragement by letters and cards. We all need heavenly balm to soften the memories of *death in the hills*.

As tears flowed, I turned off the computer and bowed my head. *Why, Lord, Why?*

Crying for God
Carol Anne Eby

The hot, tropical sun beat down upon the women as they filed into the church. With a sigh of relief, most sank down upon the low platform that served as a pew, enjoying the coolness of the stone church's interior. An hour spent in this meeting meant a release from the drudgery of digging sweet potatoes from the garden miles from their home, beating clothes upon rocks in the river, or tediously sorting and drying coffee beans. I knew this hour was a precious gift to these women, and as a young, inexperienced missionary, I wanted this time to be meaningful to them.

It was Good Friday, the first we had experienced in our missionary assignment. Teaching a Bible lesson from John 3:16, I had prepared many hours to express God's love significantly in the trade language, Melanesian Pidgin, which still had to be translated into these women's vernacular language. As I gazed at my audience of 94 women, I felt so inadequate for the task. How would I ever communicate effectively to them? I had prepared my mind, but I was soon to find out that my heart and emotions were woefully unprepared for what was to follow.

Dry-eyed, almost casually, I began a story so old to me but brand new to these women only recently introduced to the Christian message. As I showed large, colorful pictures and related the story, the women began to react rather strangely. Several began to rock back and forth, groaning and moaning a low wail that I recognized as part of their mourning ritual. Others pulled their hair and covered their faces with their string bags normally used as carryalls for everything from sweet potatoes to babies. Tears flowed freely; yet, I did not understand why they were so moved. Afraid that I had been offensive in some way, I anxiously turned to my interpreter. "What did I say? Have I offended them?"

Their hands revealed the tragic marks of heathen mourning.

"Oh, missionary," she said, "they are not offended. They are grieving for God in the loss of His only Son. They know what it means to lose a child. Look at their hands." Then I remembered another part of the mourning ritual. A bereaved mother would grasp a sharp piece of bamboo and chop a finger to the first knuckle to memorialize her child.

I glanced at the women surrounding me on the platform, and then as I began walking down the aisle, pressing hands reached up to me. Blinded by my tears, I was overcome with sorrow for these dear

The hand of a woman in Papua New Guinea
whose fingers have been cut off

women who knew what it meant to lose a son—yes, many sons. Their hands revealed the tragic marks of heathen mourning as several women had two, three, even four fingertips missing. These women truly empathized with God in a way I never had. A love that inspired such a gift to them was almost beyond comprehension, but once realized that love freed them from their bondage.

Many of those women left class that day, redeemed and transformed into living witnesses of that great love. They possessed a zeal to tell others and went from garden to garden, telling the story. Many took their lanterns and trudged the mountain trails at night to share God's redeeming love around campfires.

And because of those wise, compassionate women, I never took for granted again those blessed words: "For God so loved the world, that he gave his only begotten son . . ." (John 3:16, KJV).

From the Depths of Despair

Carol Anne Eby

"Mi laik go bek long asples bilong mi!" This phrase in Melanesian Pidgin means, "I'm ready to give up and go home."

This saying almost became my battle cry before our second furlough from mission service in Papua New Guinea. I had loved being a missionary. I loved this tropical Pacific island that had truly become home and the Tongeii people who had truly become family. God had blessed our ministry, and life was good. I couldn't believe how I had been filled with discouragement to the point I was ready to give up and go home. Discouragement can eat away at one's soul until one is filled with self-pity and resentment that breed bitterness. And nothing is quite as destructive to Kingdom work as a bitter missionary. I still feel the pain of remembering.

During our second term, because we couldn't expand at our present location, we moved from our cozy station at Tun to 80 acres of land on the main highway stretching across the Western Highlands.

Here a Bible college was established that serves over a hundred students today.

Some months before our furlough, Maria Wara, our first Christian convert, bounced up on my front porch one morning, leading a lovely young girl by the hand and introduced me to Ki, her new daughter-in-law and wife of her youngest son, Kum. Kum was the link that had brought Maria in touch with the Nazarenes. He had been quite ill as a baby, and she had taken him to the new missionary Sidney Knox, who had given the infant medicine. The baby survived, and the church had Maria's gratitude and loyalty thereafter. She walked 19 miles round-trip each Sunday to church at Kudjip and kept begging

Maria Wara

the mission to come to her area. In 1963 we arrived to fulfill that desire.

Ki and I became good friends, and before long she prayed in an evening service. Maria proudly brought her to baptismal class and declared that her daughter-in-law was following the Lord. Ki's sparkling eyes shone, and her happy smile gave evidence to her newfound faith. An active participant in the young girls' Sunday School class, Ki was an eager student. Even though preliterate, she had a burning desire to learn.

When we moved to the new Bible school location, Kum and Ki came to enroll. Never had I seen her so happy, for now she was in school every day, constantly searching for knowledge. Her progress in class was amazing. We soon noticed, however, that Kum's commitment to the Lord and his studies was halfhearted, and we feared we couldn't keep him in school. After some severe rule infractions, school officials decided to dismiss him. The problem was how to break the news to Ki.

Ki's reserve broke, and she dissolved into heartbreaking sobs.

One Sunday we went back to Tun for service, and afterward several Bible school students from that area piled into the bus to go back to school. Ki had put her string bag and saucepan into the bus and was climbing in when my husband, Lee, gently told her, "Ki, I'm sorry, but you can't go back to school today. We're happy to have you and thrilled with your progress. But Kum is going to have to straighten up his life and strengthen his commitment to God before you can come back. We will pray for both of you and hope you can come back soon."

Flashing her bright smile, she took her things and got out of the bus. I remember her waving good-bye as we drove away.

Later, we learned that when we disappeared from view Ki's reserve broke, and she dissolved into heartbreaking sobs. For a long time she mourned. Then going to Maria's house, she got the pig rope and said, "I'm going to bring in the pigs for their evening feed." Then she disappeared.

The next morning Maria and Kum were at our door saying Ki had run away. For 10 days they searched for her, even as far as 150 miles away, but to no avail. They thought of suicide, but no one really thought she was that desperate. Finally, they decided she had gotten on a truck and gone to the big city to enter a life of prostitution. I just couldn't believe that of Ki.

Finally, the afternoon of the 10th day the news came: Ki had been found. In a grove of trees behind where our house had once stood hung her remains. It seemed impossible that people could have lived and moved in that area for 10 days and never realized she was there. But the trees were so close together with high grass growing around them that Ki was hidden from view. Only when a man saw droves of flies swarming in that area did he suspect anything.

We drove to the bridge and then walked in to the station at Tun. On that short hike, I saw the beauty as perhaps never noticed before. The sky was a perfect blue, the clouds white and fleecy, the landscape green and rich with the profusion of gorgeous flowers everywhere proclaiming God's glorious creation, but in the midst of that, the ugliness of death and despair. We could hear the wailing long before we arrived. We walked to the grove, and I lifted my eyes for one glance only. She had hung so low that her body had not been protected from the pigs and dogs.

I whirled and ran to the church, collapsing at the altar. Shaken to the depths emotionally and spiritually, in that moment I felt like a complete failure, like blaming anyone who had given this young girl

Mourning ceremony in Papua New Guinea

hope, only to have it snatched away. I resented everything. *Why had the Knoxes ever come?* I anguished. *Why hadn't God done something? I wished I'd never come, had never been a missionary. O God, I can't carry this load of guilt.* I cried all the way home and all that night. Then I pulled an iron curtain down on that experience and my emotions and went on with life.

When we came back from furlough, it was a discouraging time for the Tun church. The Bible school had moved; the other missionaries had left; the buildings had been removed; the pastor and congregation were disheartened; and I was wishing to be anyplace else but here. That's not a winning combination for progress. I found myself going to the Tun services and starting to cry about the time they took the offering and continuing until I got home.

In the midst of this personal Gethsemane experience, I listened to a tape from Pasadena, California, First Church. Pastor Earl Lee (now deceased) was preaching on the "Goliaths in Our Lives," and I knew I had to do something about my Goliath of discouragement or my missionary career was over. I pulled up the iron curtain on my heartbreak over Ki and let the Lord cleanse me of it all.

I do know that Jesus is Lord of the Church, and I do know that the answer to every emotional need is in Him. I'm grateful He not only lifts souls from the depths of sin—He can lift *from the depths of despair.*

Because of God's Love
Tom Riley

The African sun blazed down on the Endzingeni Nazarene mission station. The assembly of the
Northern Swaziland District was in its second day.
The tabernacle, which Fairy Chism and Louise Rob-
inson Chapman had built with the help of an Irish
master mason, was only air-conditioned by the small
breezes that wafted in through the open windows
from time to time. To add to the humidity's annoy-
ance, the dust from the freshly-cut grass spread over
the back section of the building made even those
not normally troubled by allergies very uncomfort-
able. Removable corrugated iron panels, six feet
high, made a sleeping area for the lady delegates at
the rear of the tabernacle. Once in a while children's
cries could be heard over the privacy screen. It was
time for the morning break from the assembly busi-
ness—time to get some fresh air. The closest shade
covered the walls surrounding Harmon Schmelzenbach's grave.

Harmon and Lula, along with their children, became the first Nazarene missionaries to Africa in
1912. Alongside his grave were those of three of
their four children who died in Africa. The fourth

Harmon Schmelzenbach's grave at Endzingeni

was buried at Piggs Peak mission station about 12 miles away. When the Schmelzenbachs arrived in Swaziland, they were so short of food that their surviving son, Elmer, was given sugar to lick to keep him from crying from hunger. A local family saw the struggle the missionary family faced and gave them a cow, whose milk was credited by Elmer with saving the lives of the remaining children.

The message of Christian holiness was not an easy "pill" to take.

Planting gospel seed in Swaziland was not an easy task, but the Schmelzenbachs faithfully worked to spread the message of salvation and live a holy life. No opposition kept them from their goal, not even attacks by hostile families, who set fires to valuable thatch grass collected and stored for roofs. Conflict also came to them from harboring young girls, who, against their will, had been forced to marry much older polygamous men. When a patrol of Swazi warriors came to remove the girls by force, Harmon stood in the doorway and told the spear-carrying soldiers, "You'll have to kill me first." The warriors left and reported the incident to King Sobhuza II, who told them to give up because they were dealing with a crazy white man. Many of those young girls went on to become faithful pastors who started churches all over the country.

The name "Schmelzenbach" was not a familiar name nor easy for most Swazis to pronounce. Following Swazi custom, they gave him a name fitting of his work—Sibaha, a popular cure-all herbal medicine. Though quite bitter, the medicine had helped keep many people alive. Just like Sibaha, the message of Christian holiness was not an easy "pill" to take but gave everlasting life to those who accepted the message from God's Word.

Now, more than 50 years after Harmon's death from malaria, Swazi pastors, district superintendents, missionaries, and workers gathered around his grave. My wife, Faye, and I were among that group. Arriving in January 1968, we were assigned to Endzingeni to supervise three clinics, teach biology and English, and administer Nazarene schools in the area. It was an honor to be stationed in the area where God had first led Harmon Schmelzenbach to establish the Church of the Nazarene. Often Harmon would bring everyone together to this place under a large temporary tabernacle made of branches and thatch. The outpouring of the Holy Spirit in those meetings is still remembered.

As we rested that day in the shade of Harmon's grave, we remembered his life and work. "Look at us," District Superintendent Sibandze commented. "We are sitting at a grave site and thinking nothing about it. As Swazis we know graves are taboo, and we should not even be near one. Why is this different?"

Without hesitation pastor Richard Ginindze gave an answer: "We are sitting here so peacefully because he loved us."

All gave agreement: "Usibaha wasithanda ngempela." Schmelzenbach really loved us!

Dare to Care

Ruth Kinnersley as told to Carol Anne Eby

It was a strange mix—a retired school teacher who took up a volunteer mission career at the age of 74; Korean missionaries who were assigned to Kazakstan, once called the steppes of Russia; a converted muezzin who had once climbed up to give the call to prayer to the Muslim faithful. Daring to care was the common thread that wove their lives together.

Ruth Kinnersley retired from teaching at the age of 71 to care for her invalid husband. After her husband's death, she decided in the summer of 1996 that the Lord was not finished with her yet, and mission opportunities abounded in volunteer service. Her view of ministry had always been, "Well, I never thought of work at church as actually work." Ministry was pure joy to her; no job was too small. Caring took her to Romania, Papua New Guinea, Guatemala, Russia, Madagascar, Trinidad, and Kazakstan. Missionaries and nationals soon found that Ruth eagerly and willingly did whatever was required, never complaining about the conditions in which she found herself.

Kazakstan's barren, windswept countryside and biting cold winds reminds Ruth of North Dakota where she had lived in former days. Kazakstan, one of the former Soviet republics, stretching from the Caspian Sea to China, is about the size of the United States east of the Mississippi. While most of the land is covered with prairie grass, in the south it becomes desert, and to the southeast where it borders Afghanistan, mountainous.

Though mainly a Moslem country, Kazakstan has been tolerant of other groups. After the terrorist attacks on September 11, 2001, the government supported the United States. At the end of World War II, Stalin moved large groups of Germans there as well as Koreans to settle the steppes and increase production from that area. God's plan was unfolding.

Who better to minister to Koreans in Kazakstan than Korean missionaries. Michael and Do Yea Park with their teenage children, Young Min and Chen Song, cared very much for their own people so far from home. After serving first in Moscow, the Parks then opened the work for the Church of the Nazarene in Astana, the capital of Kazakstan, in 1996. Astana is an attractive city with wide streets and fountains and monuments in abundance. Government buildings, museums, and concert halls are all new and impressive. Kazakstan's resource of oil has made all of this possible, but the wealth of the city is in sharp contrast with many of the people who are desperately poor.

The Parks have reached out to the Korean people, many of them university students, as well as the Kazakhs. A commodious church building constructed by a Work and Witness team, houses a congrega-

First Church of the Nazarene in Kazakstan

tion of 125. Michael usually preaches in Korean with translation into Russian.

One day Ruth overheard Michael say, "Oh, I love my church," and his love shows in his dedication to ministry and care for the people. Michael uses university students to sing, play instruments, operate the overhead projector, and read the Scripture. These young people, so sincere, bow their heads in prayer before the service and take notes during Bible studies and sermons.

"The beauty and tradition of Korean worship has transferred to the Kazakstan church," Ruth says. "During Communion a professional violinist often plays the entire time, the choir wears robes, and Michael and the four young men who assist him wear vestments and white gloves. Truly a dignified and spiritual service."

*The fervor Almaz once used in calling
the Muslim faithful to prayer is
put into witnessing.*

The Parks reached out to Almaz, a Kazakh young man who had left his Muslim faith to follow Jesus. The fervor Almaz once used in calling the Muslim faithful to prayer is put into witnessing and showing the *JESUS* film. Almaz cares deeply for all those who don't know Christ.

The young man often drove Ruth to her ESL (English as a second language) classes at Faith Church on the edge of the city. She worked with some of the poor women who longed to learn English. One day after class, Ruth asked Almaz to take her to Do Yea's home. Ruth wanted to send an E-mail to her family. When they arrived, Do Yea introduced them to a man who was remodeling the apartment. When Ruth went into the other room to use the computer, Almaz stayed to chat with the worker.

When Ruth finished, Do Yea asked, "Won't you have some tea?"

"Oh, you don't need to fix tea for me," Ruth responded, not wanting to intrude any more on her time.

Do Yea whispered, "Almaz is telling the worker about the Lord."

"Then some tea is just what I need," Ruth responded.

Almaz and Do Yea Park

On the way home, Ruth asked Almaz about the encounter. "I presented the four spiritual laws," he said, "but the man isn't quite ready to accept the message. But I'm not discouraged at all. We'll keep after him. I think this remodeling will take a long time. We'll go back!"

Perhaps the mix isn't so strange after all. A retired grandmother, two dedicated missionaries, and a fervent witness blended together in a potpourri of caring outpoured on people who truly need the Lord.

Passing Through the Waters

Carol Anne Eby

I scanned the horizon anxiously as our family piled into the Land Rover headed to our main station at Kudjip. Well into the rainy season, we could set our watches by the regularity of afternoon deluges. We hoped to make the trip speedily, picking up supplies and returning before our mountain road turned into a river of mud and the river near our home turned into a roaring torrent. Since it was the week before Christmas, the anticipation of gifts and goodies awaiting us probably clouded our judgment. And the pleas of two plaintive toddlers also moved us to action.

We arrived at Kudjip to find stacks of boxes and bags that had been flown in from the coast to fill our six-month shopping list. Our mission colleagues helped us pack the car to the brim and invited us in for coffee. As the heavens opened up about that time, we decided it was too stormy to travel, so we enjoyed early Christmas treats and the warm fellowship we often missed on our isolated station.

When the storm abated, we headed home to

Tun, hoping the worst was over. The road was slippery but passable, and everything was fine until we reached the ford in the river. Normally, the water was at ankle level and a great place for the women to beat their clothes on the rocks as they did the weekly laundry. The river was even shallow enough to bathe their babies and wash dishes. Our children loved to wade there and play among the rocks.

My husband, Lee, began the crossing. Though the water was running fast, it didn't look that deep. Arriving in the middle, suddenly the front of the Land Rover took a nosedive. Evidently the torrential rains had washed out the ford. The engine died, and no coaxing would start it again.

Just then I looked up the river, and around the curve was coming a wall of water. We were trapped!

The river ford at Tun washed out

Lee opened the door on the downstream side, but the current was too swift to step out. Our children were both under four, and I had weak ankles. I was afraid we would be unable to stand in the water. Lee stood in the doorway of the vehicle and began to yell for help. As raindrops began to beat on top of the car, Lee's yells reverberated through the storm. Baby Lee Ann giggled with delight as she patted the window, watching the waters rise. Her older brother, Mark, sobbed in terror as he stared at the flood. My voice trembled as I prayed aloud and reminded the Lord of His promise, "When you pass through the waters, I will be with you; and when you pass through the rivers, they will not sweep over you" (Isa. 43:2*a*).

— . — . — . — . —

The men came running with sturdy ropes, strong arms, and sure feet to triumph over the raging flood.

— . — . — . — . —

Unknown to us, the Bible school students and people from the local village who had seen our vehicle die in the river began to mourn our certain death. Then a miracle happened. Through all that noise, our Papuan carpenters, up from the coast to build our new church, heard our pleas for help. The men came running with sturdy ropes, strong arms, and sure feet to triumph over the raging flood. Unlike our Highlanders who were terrified of the water, they were familiar with coastal waters and ocean currents and unafraid to match themselves against nature's fury. The men rushed into the swirling current, picked the children and me up, and carried us to safety—but back to the riverbank from which we'd come. After the men assisted Lee, our family found shelter in a nearby home. The men tied ropes around the drifting vehicle and secured them to trees along the shore. Now, the river had turned into a roaring torrent carrying everything in its path—huge logs, banana trees, squealing pigs. Hours later when the waters receded, we walked across to our home. Bible school students unloaded the vehicle, still partially submerged, and carried all the sodden boxes to our front hall.

The next day in the eerie calm of the early dawn we went back to investigate the damage. The ropes had held, and although the waters swept through the vehicle all night, it had not been lost to the flood. A few eggs floating in the water and some wrapped candies lodged in the muddy bank would be delightful surprises for future scavengers. We had gained a new respect for the power of water and a renewed faith in God who had brought us safely through the flooded ford.

Praying for Chicago
Geneva Silvernail

The younger children sat on grass mats near the altar to leave space on the pews for the adults. In the back of the church on other mats, I noticed the grandmothers sitting with their legs stretched out in front of them. The bottoms of their feet showed deep cracks caused by years of walking barefoot on the rocky trails around their village.

Just as the service was about to begin, a young lady entered. Somehow, I moved over and made room for her on our already crowded bench. It was mission Sunday, and the church was packed. After the music time, the speaker, our own local missionary president, walked to the pulpit.

We leaned forward, our ears straining to hear her soft voice. She spoke the words again, but this time more forcefully, "Chicago, Chicago." The young men on the left side of the church repeated, "Chicago, Chicago." Then the young ladies on the right side picked up the swishing sound and steady rhythm as if a train would soon begin its journey. Soon the entire congregation repeated, "Chicago, Chicago," until the words had their own melody, stirring chords of excitement and interest in each listener.

"Thrust to the City," the speaker said emphatically. The missionary president spoke of the needs of the people in a faraway country where they did not have good homes or food like those in Swaziland. She described the homeless and jobless. She explained that there were few Nazarene churches in Chicago, and people had to meet in stores just to worship. Tears came to her eyes as she raised her head and declared with a loud voice that the people in Chicago needed the Lord. The congregation responded with the rhythmic, "Chicago, Chicago."

The speaker challenged the congregation to attend a special prayer meeting to pray for the needs of Chicago. I attended the service, but while others interceded, I found it difficult to pray for Chicago. She had spoken of the needs of Chicago, yet I remembered she was speaking to people who lived in grass-thatched-roof homes with mud-plastered walls and no electricity or water . . . to professionals who lived in cement-block homes with corrugated-iron roofs . . . to grandmothers and grandfathers who had never ridden in a private car or spoken on a telephone . . . to children who had a high chance of dying from childhood diseases . . . to mothers who cooked on wood-burning stoves and carried their water supply on their heads from the river.

— · — · — · — · —

As I squirmed trying to get comfortable, the Lord finally captured my attention.

— · — · — · — · —

As I listened to the prayers around me, I felt that the needs of Chicago were nothing compared to the needs of my friends in Swaziland. Nevertheless, I began to pray. Minutes later, I was checking the time. Where did they find all those words to pray for just one little request? I lay my head down on my left arm, then on my right, then down on both arms. I wiggled and put my feet straight out in front of me, then I crossed them at the ankles. I sat on the left leg, and then on the right one, and then knelt on both knees.

As I squirmed trying to get comfortable, the Lord finally captured my attention. "Geneva, you are not interested in missions," He whispered.

I could not believe it. I, a missionary, not interested in missions? Could the Lord have me mixed up with someone else? Why, I had come all the way to Africa, leaving family, friends, and many conveniences of home. I had spent long hours studying the culture and the language of Swaziland. I suffered emotionally when my son, David, left for Trevecca Nazarene University, daughter Debbie for Point Loma Nazarene University, and daughter Denise for the boarding home in South Africa. I argued, but the Lord seemed to whisper again, "Really, My child, you are not interested in missions."

God showed me I was interested only in my own little world in Swaziland, only concerned with their needs. My enthusiasm for missions was only where I lived and not for the world. I had no vision.

I slowly accepted what God was telling me. I realized that all my time, energy, and prayers were centered on the Swazi people. In earnest, I began to pray for the faraway place called Chicago. I soon forgot about the cement floor, about numb feet and aching legs. I prayed for those in spiritual darkness in Chicago. I became interested in missions. Perhaps, that was the moment I became a *real* missionary.

Stuck in the Muck
Tim Eby

As I bounced down the bumpy road made from sharp lava rocks, I observed that people continued their normal routines. Children played hopscotch in the dirt. Young boys pushed wooden bicycles laden with bags of rice down the road. Mothers sat in the afternoon heat on the side of the road with a small plastic tarp spread on the ground where their wares were displayed for sale. I sat in the front of the dinky little truck next to our local district superintendent Rev. Bailbanga, while in the back numerous pastors clung to the rails to keep from being tossed from the truck's bed.

We crested the little hill next to the Goma airport on our way to the Nazarene church and primary school settled in Majengo, a suburb of Goma. What came into view stunned me beyond comprehension. On normal trips to this place, visited many times before, we would find more than 300 children dressed in white and blue uniforms, singing and dancing around our vehicle. Flowers would be presented by young girls as gifts to the visitors with carefully recited words of welcome. Many handshakes and smiles would warm our hearts as we watched teachers present their classes one by one with choral verses and songs of inspiration.

Today there would be no singing. No dancing. No children. Not even a building or the remains thereof. I stretched my eyes across the horizon only to see mounds of lava rocks piled into heaps as though they had been tossed from the mountain like trash. Smoke filled the air, and ash dropped lightly from the sky. Among the twisted rock and molten lava lay remnants of a society that once stood there. Rusted shells of vehicles lay trapped in the rock with everything burned from the tires to the steering wheel. Plates and forks stood in the rock as though they had been stuck in porridge and left there to rot. A steeple of a Catholic church lay on its side just above the rock, the building destroyed. Burned banana stalks rimmed the edge of the rock mass, and partial portions of cement-brick houses lay in random heaps among the rubble.

I stepped out on the rocks to make my way across the river of cooling lava. Hot spots still belched plumes of smoke, and the heat fogged my glasses. The smell of sulfur hung in the air, thick enough to almost touch. I took deep breaths for oxygen and covered my mouth with a handkerchief. The soles of my shoes were getting hotter as I noticed children digging through the rubble. They carried burned sheet metal from the wreckage to build temporary shelters just to survive. The pastors shook their heads in dismay and stared into the afternoon sky, wondering if God would have mercy on them. The things that once identified their life, the very essence of everything they could call their own, now

Tim Eby on location in Africa

lay somewhere deep beneath the surface of the earth encased forever by a lava river that had swept and burned everything away.

As I stumbled across the rocks back toward our vehicle, I came across a 55-gallon drum completely submerged in hardened rock, except for one protruding corner. The drum was complete yet tarnished by the heat. It had held its shape even in the midst of the tumultuous upheaval of the earth. I beat on its side. The container was tough—resisting everything though trapped in time, never again to be removed from its black solid encasement of rock. I pondered the site of the drum for just a moment—truly *stuck in the muck!* It seemed so simple yet so symbolic of what I have observed about this area of the world.

Year after year missionaries travel to the deep heart of Africa, hoping to free it from the grip of Satan. We come with programs, well intentioned, but sometimes inappropriate for the culture. NGOs (nongovernmental organizations) rush to every humanitarian crisis to bring relief to the suffering. Churches with long histories of religious protocol and ritualistic practices exchange their methods of worship with heathen societies following ancestral spiritual worship with no change of the heart. Their "priests" take the places of the witch doctors of the past and preach prosperity and wealth to those who will follow their religion.

— · — · — · — · —

"Why am I here?" I began to ask God.
"What good can I do in this place?"

— · — · — · — · —

After all the good intentions, after all the Western ideas of education and social development, we return each year to see our people still struggling to survive. Barely keeping their heads above starvation, they are only a breath away from being swallowed into the sea of humanity. They pass from this life to the next by the thousands due to disease and despair each day. Forgotten by the important powers of the West and trodden on by their own leaders for personal gain, they are truly sunk just as deep as that

55-gallon drum in the rock. Africa still seems to be *stuck in the muck!*

That evening after eating a good meal and washing my face and hands with clean water, I went to my room. Under the light of a kerosene lantern, I knelt by my bed on the grass mat covering the cement floor. Images of our church people flashed through my mind as I imagined them running in the night, trying to flee the flood of fire rolling through this town. I wondered what kind of pain must have been felt by the relatives of Shadrack, a Nazarene, who had crawled into a cave, thinking the lava would not harm him, only to perish from the suffocating gases and intense heat.

"Why am I here?" I began to ask God. "What good can I do in this place? My resources are so limited and so are the churches. O God, what can help these people climb out of the miry clay? What can I do to be a witness of God's love in a place where all hope seems to be gone?"

While the sun was still climbing over the volcanic mountain and spreading itself into the valley for a new day, I awoke to the sound of drums. Voices rose from beyond the walls of my room with joy and exultation. Could it really be the Christians in our church praying and singing praises to our God? The prayer was a din of people shouting to their God, thanking Him for seeing them through another night and beseeching the Father to help them in this time of need. They shouted in Swahili until the whole neighborhood could hear them. *How can these people still face the new day with hope in their God when things seemed so hopeless?* I thought to myself. But who was I to doubt my God's ability to cope with human frailty?

The lost of Africa will be saved not by our wisdom or strength, but only by the Spirit of God who loves the lost, gives comfort to the lonely, and brings healing to the brokenhearted. I need not worry about the answers to all the questions unfolding before me but simply bring people in touch with the Master's hand. One by one He pulls sinners from being *stuck in the muck*. There is hope in Christ.

Pronunciation Guide

The following information is provided to assist in pronouncing some unfamiliar words in this book. The suggested pronunciations, though not always precise, are close approximations of the way the terms are pronounced.

Afrikaans	af-ree-KAHNS
Afrikaner	af-ree-KAH-ner
Almaz	ahl-MAHZ
Astana	ah-STAH-nah
Bailbanga	bah-eel-BAHN-gah
Banz	BAHNZ
Bajoyo	bah-HOH-yoh
catadores	kat-uh-DOH-rays
Cyangugu	sie-ahn-GOO-goo
Durban	DER-buhn
Endzingeni	ehn-dzihn-GEH-nee
Ginindze	gee-NEE-dzee
Goma	GOH-muh
Ihombe	ee-HOHM-bay
Kazakstan	kaz-ak-STAN
Kazakh	kuh-ZAK
Ki	KEE
Kigala	kee-GAH-lah
Kivu	KEE-voo
Kudjip	KOO-jihp
Kum	KOOM
Kwisha	KWEE-shah

Luzia	loo-ZEE-ah
Majengo	mah-JAYN-goh
Manzini	mahn-ZEE-nee
Mbeya	mm-BAY-yah
Melanesian	mehl-uh-NEE-zhuhn
muezzin	moo-EH-zuhn
Olinda	oh-LEEN-duh
Park, Do Yea	PAHK DOH YEH
Chen Song	CHEHN SOHNG
Young Min	YUHNG MIHN
Pietermaritzburg	PEE-ter-MAHR-uhts-berg
Recife	ray-SEE-fay
Salome	say-LOH-may
Sibaha	see-BAH-hah
Sibandze	see-BAHN-dzee
Tongeii	tohng-AY
Tun	TOON
Wara	WAH-rah

Mi laik go bek long asples bilong mi.
MEE LIEK GOH BEHK LAHNG AHS-plays
BEE-lahng MEE

Usibaha wasithanda ngempela.
oo-see-BAH-ha wah-seet-HAHN-dah
n-gaym-PAY-lah